THE WORK OF BRUCE McALLISTER

MORE WILDSIDE CLASSICS

Please see www.wildsidepress.com for a complete list!

THE WORK OF BRUCE McALLISTER

An Annotated Bibliography & Guide

by

DAVID RAY BOURQUIN

WILDSIDE PRESS

For Bonnie, Tim, and Emile

THE WORK OF BRUCE McALLISTER

This edition published in 2006 by Wildside Press, LLC.
www.wildsidepress.com

CONTENTS

INTRODUCTION

Bruce Hugh McAllister was born on October 17, 1946 in Baltimore, Maryland. He grew up in the behavioral sciences and marine sciences, with his mother an archeologist, anthropologist, and educator, and his father a career Naval officer and professor of ocean engineering. Life in a military family meant constant relocations, and McAllister spent a colorful, peripatetic childhood in settings as diverse as Florida, California, Washington, D.C., and Italy.

Each of these elements from McAllister's background has left its indelible mark on his writing, especially his science fiction. Anthropology, psychology and marine biology are the sciences most often treated in his science fiction, and California and Italy have provided the settings for many of his better-known works. His universal vision of humanity, his interest in the theme of "the alien" in science fiction, and even his very attraction to science fiction itself are, he admits, inevitable reflections of his experience in a family accustomed to mobility and cross-cultural perspectives.

McAllister is not just a science fiction writer, however; he is also a poet, writer of literary fiction, editor, and successful academic. He graduated from Claremont Men's College in 1969 with a B.A. in English, after having experimented with five undergraduate majors. During that period he worked briefly as a process server, Disneyland busboy, ranch hand, and UPI sports rewriter in New York City, and pursued a television writing major at UCLA for one quarter. His Master of Fine Arts degree in fiction writing was completed at the University of California, Irvine, in 1971. His thesis was a science fiction novel, *Humanity Prime*, probably the first time a science fiction novel had ever been used for an MFA degree in the U.S.

Since 1971 he has taught at the University of Redlands, where he directs the Writing Program and English Internship Program, which places student interns in a variety of actual working situations for academic credit. He received tenure in 1980 and became full Professor of English in 1983. He has also taught courses in science fiction and literature at other institutions in southern California, and has spoken widely to colleges, high schools, and interested groups. He is a writing strategist in the field of disaster policy, a consultant in technical writing and public relations, and a freelance article writer as well.

I asked Bruce about his reading and writing interests, and the answers proved illuminating. Like many SF authors, he began reading and writing science fiction at an early age, and wrote his first published story ("The Faces Outside," *If*, 1963) at sixteen. Among his early reading interests were Ray Bradbury, A. E. van Vogt, Arthur C. Clarke, Clifford Simak, Harlan Ellison and Andre Norton. He characterizes the science fiction he has written over the past two decades as dominated by psychological, medical,anthropological, and theological themes, and is especially interested in the question of "what it means to be human" and in the role of "the alien" in science fiction. His protagonists are often human beings faced with enormous challenges and all-too-human limits who succeed only by transcendence or revelation of one kind or another.

McAllister confesses that he spent most of the 1970's writing poetry and experimental fiction and editing literary quarterlies, but that he has returned to science fiction to stay. His new work within the field, however, may be the beneficiary of that hiatus; within the field he is known as a stylist and "literary" science fiction writer. His current reading interests include William Golding, Dashiell Hammett, Pär Lagerkvist, Ursula K. Le Guin, and the short story masters of science fiction.

He lives in Redlands with his wife Caroline, a photographer, and their daughter Annie and son Ben, all of whom enjoy traveling, other cultures, and the sea.

I wish to thank Bruce for his assistance with this biography, and especially for our very pleasant evening on May 14, 1985, during which he patiently answered my many questions.

—David Ray Bourquin
Redlands, California
Nov. 28, 1985

BOOKS

A1. *Humanity Prime*. New York: Ace Books, 1971, 285 p., paper. [novel]

The descendants of a handful of human survivors finally meet the alien race which all but annihilated mankind three thousand years ago. The cyborg starship which brought the aquatic survivors to the water-covered planet Prime now lies on an island, crippled and insane. The survivors, now mutated merpeople, communicate telepathically, procreate by a kind of parthenogenesis, and inhabit a non-verbal, non-mechanical society permeated by three thousand years of very conscious racial memories. As the story opens, a probe ship from the reptilian Cromanths lands on Prime. The protagonist, the orphan boy Fishsinger, must confront the aliens accompanied only by his pet and by his father's friend, a wise, turtle-like being. In the end Fishsinger defeats the Cromanths, but must choose between psychic union with the cyborg or a more "human" life as a merboy in the bright oceans of Prime.

REVIEWS:

1. "Review of *Humanity Prime*," in *Futures: The Journal of Forecasting and Planning* 3 (December, 1971): 415-416.
2. "Of *Humanity Prime*," in *Science Fiction News* (December, 1971): 3-5.
3. *Learning for Tomorrow: The Role of the Future in Education*, edited by Alvin Toffler. New York: Vintage Books, 1974, paper, p. 246.

A2. *Poems: Massman, Costanzo, McAllister*, by Gordon Massman, Gerald Costanzo, and Bruce McAllister. Reno, NV: West Coast Poetry Review Press, 1973, 65 p., paper. [collection]

A tri-authored poetry collection containing a selection of original poems by the author, under the collective title "Rising Rooms." The individual poems include: "Suffocation," "Poem (Marilyn)," "Seeing Red," "First Fish or Woman," "Jealousy," "Found Vocal No. 4," "Two Reasons We Should Keep On," "Vacation," "Poem (Old Woman)," "Upkeep," "Aging," "A Myth of Ambergris," and "Man-O-War."

A3. *Their Immortal Hearts: Three Visions of Time*, edited anonymously by Bruce McAllister. Reno, NV: West Coast Poetry Review, 1980, 168 p., paper. [anthology]

An anthology of three short novels: "Cold War Orphans," by Michael Bishop (p. 7-36); "Le Croix (The Cross)," by Barry N. Malzberg (p. 37-78); and "Their Immortal Hearts," by Bruce McAllister (p. 79-164). All deal with the theme of immortality.

FORTHCOMING BOOKS:

A4.   *The Faces Outside.*   San Bernardino, CA: The Borgo Press, 1986,   p., cloth (published simultaneously in trade paperback). [collection]

A collection of the author's short stories, with an introduction by Gregory Benford.

A5.   *Naming the Stars: The Book of Science Fiction Poetry*, edited by Bruce McAllister and Dick Allen; introduction by Arthur C. Clarke. [anthology]

An anthology of science fiction poetry.

A6.   *Their Immortal Hearts.*   An expansion of the novella into novel form.

A7.   *Humanity Prime.* A revision.

A8.   *Dream Baby.* An expansion of the novelette into novel form.

A9.   *Kin.* A novel.

SHORT FICTION

B1. "The Faces Outside," in *If: Worlds of Science Fiction* 13 (July, 1963): 57-63.

    b. *The 9th Annual of the Year's Best SF*, edited by Judith Merril. New York: Simon & Schuster, 1964, cloth, p. 109-119.

    bb. *The 9th Annual of the Year's Best SF*, edited by Judith Merril. New York: Dell Books, 1965, paper, p. 109-119.

    c. as: "Le Facce Dietro il Vetro," in *Urania* no. 364 (Dec. 27, 1964): 78-87. [Italian]

B2. "We Hunters of Men," in *If: Worlds of Science Fiction* 15 (August, 1965): 39-62.

B3. "Gods of the Dark and Light," in *If: Worlds of Science Fiction* 17 (February, 1967): 49-56.

    b. as: "Gli Dei del Buio e della Luce," in *Urania* no. 491 (June 16, 1968): 63-74. [Italian]

B4. "Without a Doubt Dream," in *The Magazine of Fantasy and Science Fiction* 34 (April, 1968): 46-54.

    b. as: "Cauchemar de Sabel," in *Fiction* no. 248 (August, 1974): 27-39. [French]

B5. "Prime-Time Teaser," in *The Magazine of Fantasy and Science Fiction* 35 (December, 1968): 5-14.

    b. *Twenty Years of the Magazine of Fantasy and Science Fiction*, edited by Edward L. Ferman and Robert P. Mills. New York: G. P. Putnam's Sons, 1970, cloth, p. 148-158.

    bb. *Twenty Years of the Magazine of Fantasy and Science Fiction*, edited by Edward L. Ferman and Robert P. Mills. New York: Berkley Medallion Books, 1970, paper, p. 183-195.

    c. as: "La Tortue de Mer," in *Fiction* no. 208 (April, 1971): 109-122. [French]

B6. "Benji's Pencil," in *The Magazine of Fantasy and Science Fiction* 36 (March, 1969): 120-128.

  b. *From Pop to Culture*, edited by Michael E. Malone and Myron Roberts. New York: Holt, Rinehart & Winston, 1971, paper, p. 483-493.
  c. *The Best from Fantasy and Science Fiction, Nineteenth Series*, edited by Edward L. Ferman. Garden City, NY: Doubleday & Co., 1971, cloth, p. 273-283.
  cb. *The Best from Fantasy and Science Fiction, 19th Series*, edited by Edward L. Ferman. New York: Ace Books, 1973, paper, p. 300-312.
  d. as: "Des Crayons pour Benji," in *Fiction* no. 246 (June, 1974): 35-48. [French]

B7. "The Man Inside," in *Galaxy Magazine* 28 (May, 1969): 141-143.

  b. *Best SF: 1969*, edited by Harry Harrison and Brian W. Aldiss. New York: G. P. Putnam's Sons, 1970, cloth, p. 207-210.
  bb. *Best SF: 1969*, edited by Harry Harrison and Brian W. Aldiss. New York: Berkley Medallion Books, 1971, paper, p. 192-194.
  c. *Science Fiction and Fantasy*, edited by Fred Obrecht. New York: Barron's, 1970, paper, p. 83-88.
  cb. *Science Fiction and Fantasy*, edited by Fred Obrecht. Woodbury, NY: Barron's Educational Series, 1977, paper, p. 83-84.
  d. *From Pop to Culture*, edited by Michael E. Malone and Myron Roberts. New York: Holt, Rinehart & Winston, 1971, paper, p. 207-209.
  e. *100 Great Science Fiction Short Stories*, edited by Isaac Asimov, Martin Harry Greenberg, and Joseph D. Olander. Garden City, NY: Doubleday & Co., 1978, cloth, p. 228-230.
  eb. *100 Great Science Fiction Short Stories*, edited by Isaac Asimov, Martin Harry Greenberg, and Joseph D. Olander. New York: Avon Books, 1978, paper, p. 251-253.

B8. "The Big Boy," in *Fantastic Stories* 18 (June, 1969): 78-82.

B9. "Autohuman 14," in *If: Worlds of Science Fiction* 19 (July, 1969): 61-66.

B10. "Life Matter," in *Galaxy Magazine* 128 (actually 28) (August, 1969): 97-106.

B11. "And So Say All of Us," in *If: Worlds of Science Fiction* 19 (September, 1969): 36-45.

    b. *World's Best Science Fiction 1970*, edited by Donald A. Wollheim and Terry Carr. New York: Ace Books, 1970, paper, p. 246-257.

    bb. *World's Best Science Fiction 1970*, edited by Donald A. Wollheim and Terry Carr. New York: Ace Books, 1970, cloth, p. 236-246. [book club edition]

B12. "After the Bomb Cliches," in *The Magazine of Fantasy and Science Fiction* 37 (November, 1969): 76-80.

    b. as: "Clichés Nucléaires," in *Fiction* no. 249 (September, 1974): 115-121. [French]

B13. "E Pluribus Solo," in *The Magazine of Fantasy and Science Fiction* 38 (January, 1970): 50-56.

B14. "Mother of Pearl," in *The Magazine of Fantasy and Science Fiction* 38 (June, 1970): 68-78.

B15. "The Warmest Memory," in *The Magazine of Fantasy and Science Fiction* 39 (December, 1970): 72-79.

    b. as: "Le Souvenir le Plus Ardent," in *Fiction* no. 258 (June, 1975): 135-145. [French]

B16. "World of the Wars," in *Mars, We Love You*, edited by Jane Hipolito and Willis E. McNelly. Garden City, NY: Doubleday & Co., 1971, cloth, p. 303-309. (published simultaneously in trade paperback)

    ab. *Mars, We Love You*, edited by Jane Hipolito and Willis E. McNelly. New York: Pyramid Books, 1973, paper, p. 347-353.

B17. "Ecce Femina!" in *The Magazine of Fantasy and Science Fiction* 42 (February, 1972): 117-144.

    b. *Above the Human Landscape: A Social Science Fiction Anthology*, edited by Willis E. McNelly and Leon E. Stover. Pacific Palisades, CA: Goodyear Publishing Co., 1972, paper, p. 272-299.

B18. "Triangle," in *The Magazine of Fantasy and Science Fiction* 43 (December, 1972): 99-110.

B19. "The Arrangement," in *Showcase*, edited by Roger Elwood. New York: Harper & Row, 1973, cloth, p. 102-118.

B20. "Letters Toward August," in *Inlet* 2 (n.d., 1974?): 25-28.

  b. "Letters Toward August," in *Redlands Review* 1 (Spring, 1975): 19.

B21. "From *Thank You*, a Book," in *Center* 7 (April, 1975): 10.

B22. "From *Thank You*, a Book," in *The Fault* (April, 1975): (60-61).

B23. "From *Thank You*, a Narrative," in *Snakeroots* (Fall, 1975): (35-36).

B24. "From *Thank You*, a Book," in *Corduroy* 7 (1975): 10.

B25. "'Waiting,' from *Thank You*, a Novel," in *Adios Againe*, issue no. 7 of *Lunar Retorno* (1975): 28-31.

B26. "Positioning," in *The Port Townsend Journal* 1 (Winter/Spring, 1975-1976): 1.

B27. "From *Thank You*, a Narrative," in *Greenhouse Review* 3 (Winter, 1976): 24-26.

B28. "From *Thank You*, a Book, 'The Country That Had No Name'," in *Lowland Review* 3 (Winter, 1976): 44-46.

B29. "From *Thank You*, a Narrative," in *Scree* 5 (1976): 67-69.

B30. "From *Thank You*, a Narrative," in *Wind/Literary Journal* 6 (no. 23, 1976): 68-74.

B31. "Cottage with White Picket Fence," in *Gallimaufry* 8/9 (Winter, 1977): 32-34.

B32. "From *Thank You*, a Narrative," in *Brushfire* 26 (1977): 26-27, 28-29.

B33. "Victor," in *The Magazine of Fantasy and Science Fiction* 53 (July, 1977): 96-102.

    b. *The Best Science Fiction of the Year #7*, edited by Terry Carr. New York: Ballantine Books, 1978, paper, p. 251-259.
    c. In *Fujin Gaho Sha*. [Japanese]

B34. "The Boy," in *New Worlds 10*, edited by Hilary Bailey. London: Corgi Books, 1977, paper, p. 70-84.

B35. "From *Thank You*, a Narrative," in *Wild Fennel* 14 (February, 1978): 15-16.

B36. "Why I Want This Job," in *Orangewood* 3 (Spring, 1978): 35-36.

B37. "Missionary Work," in *The Magazine of Fantasy and Science Fiction* 55 (December, 1978): 139-157.

B38. "Their Immortal Hearts," in *Their Immortal Hearts: Three Visions of Time*. Reno, NV: West Coast Poetry Review, 1980, paper, p. 79-164.

The author's major work of short fiction. Mayer Dar, a revolutionary, agrees to allow herself to be impregnated by the immortal Gaetano for the sake of a revolutionary conspiracy. She will terminate the pregnancy in time to free her planet from Gaetano, who owns her world's mineral rights, and who has for all intents and purposes enslaved her people. But the immortal tricks her and the child is born. The immortal commits suicide, and although Mayer and the genius behind the revolutionary conspiracy will now take over the immortal's empire, becoming immortals themselves, they know that they too will commit suicide at some distant time.

REVIEWS:

1. *Publishers Weekly* 217 (February 8, 1980): 79.
2. *Kirkus Reviews* 48 (March 1, 1980): 323.
3. *Washington Post Bookworld* (October 26, 1980): 7. Re-

viewed by Robert Silverberg.
4. *Foundation* no. 21 (February, 1981): 83-84. Reviewed by Brian Stableford.
5. *Los Angeles Times Book Review* (February 22, 1981): 12. Reviewed in his "Paper Weight" column by Ben Reuven.
6. *The Magazine of Fantasy and Science Fiction* 61 (July, 1981): 34. Reviewed by Thomas M. Disch.

B39. "What He Wore for Them," in *The Magazine of Fantasy and Science Fiction* 59 (August, 1980): 64-84.

B40. "When the Fathers Go," in *Universe 12*, edited by Terry Carr. Garden City, NY: Doubleday & Co., 1982, cloth, p. 81-103.

    ab. *Universe 12*, edited by Terry Carr. New York: Zebra Books, 1983, paper, p. 114-144.
    b. *The Best Science Fiction of the Year #12*, edited by Terry Carr. New York: Pocket Books, 1983, paper, p. 323-350.

B41. "The Ark," in *Omni* 7 (September, 1985): 44-51, 94-98.

B42. "Killing the Lambs of God," in *Stardate* 2 (January/February, 1986): 56-62.

FORTHCOMING STORIES:

B43. "Kingdom Come," in *Omni* 8 (August, 1986): .

B44. "Baby," in *Omni* 8 (1986): .

B45. "Dream Baby," in *In Fields of Fire*, edited by Jack Dann and Jeanne Dann. New York: Tor Books, 1986, paper, p. .

NON-FICTION

C1. "Eleven Days Without Sleep," by Randy Gardner and Bruce McAllister, in *Life* 56 (February 14, 1964): 71-72. [non-bylined article]

C2. "Films Help Career Guidance Programs," by P. E. Patterson and others (with anonymous contributions by Bruce McAllister), in *Audiovisual Instruction* 16 (May, 1971): 78-80. [article]

C3. "Do We Need This Knowledge?" in *The 8th Annual Best SF: 74*, edited by Harry Harrison and Brian Aldiss. Indianapolis: Bobbs-Merrill Co., 1975, cloth, p. 4-6. [introduction]

C4. "What Is Lost: Eugenio Montale's 'L'Anguilla'," in *Italia America* 3 (July-December, 1978): 28. [article]

C5. "Social Disorder, a Disaster Myth," by Bruce McAllister, Linda Burzotta Nilson, Douglas C. Nilson, and Richard Stuart Olson, in *Hazard Monthly* 2 (July, 1981): 1, 13. [article]

C6. "Facing Mirrors: Respecting Two Distinct Poetic Voices; a Review of the Poetry of Robert Fossum and Sy Kahn with Fossum and Kahn Excerpts," in *Current: The Public Affairs Magazine of Claremont McKenna College* 4 (Spring, 1982): 12-14. [article]

C7. "What Writers Should Know About Little Magazines," in *The Writer* 97 (March, 1984): 10-12, 45. [article]

    b. *The Writer's Handbook*, edited by Sylvia Burrack. Boston: The Writer, 1986, cloth, p. 512-516.

C8. "The Rock-Nesting Ospreys of Corsica," with Emmanuel Sailler, in *International Wildlife* (1986): .

POETRY

D1. "Meetings," in *Cave* 1 (April, 1972): 31.

D2. "Exploring Late," in *Cave* 3 (February, 1973): 46.

D3. "A Legend of Anon," in *Cave* 3 (February, 1973): 46.

D4. "Mirages," in *Poetry Venture* 5 (Spring, 1973): 29.

D5. "Stand Up," in *The Dragonfly* 4 (April, 1973): 3-4.

NOTE: The following group of poems, D6-D18, had the collective title "Rising Rooms."

D6. "Aging," in *Poems: Massman, Costanzo, McAllister.* Reno, NV: West Coast Poetry Review, 1973, paper, p. 57.

D7. "First Fish or Woman," in *Poems: Massman, Costanzo, McAllister.* Reno, NV: West Coast Poetry Review, 1973, paper, p. 51.

D8. "Found Vocal No. 4," in *Poems: Massman, Costanzo, McAllister.* Reno, NV: West Coast Poetry Review, 1973, paper, p. 53.

D9. "Jealousy," in *Poems: Massman, Costanzo, McAllister.* Reno, NV: West Coast Poetry Review, 1973, paper, p. 52.

D10. "Man-O-War," in *Poems: Massman, Costanzo, McAllister.* Reno, NV: West Coast Poetry Review, 1973, paper, p. 59.

D11. "A Myth of Ambergris," in *Poems: Massman, Costanzo, McAllister.* Reno, NV: West Coast Poetry Review, 1973, paper, p. 58.

D12. "Poem" (Marilyn), in *Poems: Massman, Costanzo, McAllister.* Reno, NV: West Coast Poetry Review, 1973, paper, p. 49.

D13. "Poem" (Old Woman), in *Poems: Massman, Costanzo, McAllister.* Reno, NV: West Coast Poetry Review, 1973, paper, p. 55.

D14. "Seeing Red," in *Poems: Massman, Costanzo, McAllister.* Reno, NV: West Coast Poetry Review, 1973, paper, p. 50.

D15. "Suffocation," in *Poems: Massman, Costanzo, McAllister.* Reno, NV: West Coast Poetry Review, 1973, paper, p. 48.

D16. "Two Reasons We Should Keep On," in *Poems: Massman, Costanzo, McAllister.* Reno, NV: West Coast Poetry Review, 1973, paper, p. 54.

D17. "Upkeep," in *Poems: Massman, Costanzo, McAllister.* Reno, NV: West Coast Poetry Review, 1973, paper, p. 56.

D18. "Vacation," in *Poems: Massman, Costanzo, McAllister.* Reno, NV: West Coast Poetry Review, 1973, paper, p. 54.

D19. "Fossil," in *The Windless Orchard* 22 (Summer, 1975): 20.

D20. "Breasts," in *Icarus, a Poetry Journal* 4 (Winter, 1976): 18-19.

D21. "The Retarded Boy Our Parents Should Have Had," in *Poetry Northwest* 17 (Summer, 1976): 33-34.

D22. "The Last Man and Supper," in *College English* 38 (February, 1977): 589.

D23. "Marilyn Monroe," in *Rendezvous* 12 (Spring, 1977): 37.

D24. "Aligning Constellations and Pets," in *Prism International* 16 (Fall, 1977): 64.

D25. "Partial Memory," in *Prism International* 16 (Fall, 1977): 63.

D26. "Poem," in *Prism International* 16 (Fall, 1977): 65.

D27. "Poem on Your Teaching," in *Zahir* 9 (issue 2, 1977): 60.

D28. "First and Last Contact," in *Rocket Candy*, edited by Duane Ackerson. Salem, OR: The Dragonfly Press, 1977, paper, p. 62-63.

   b. *The Umbral Anthology of Science Fiction Poetry*, edited by Steve Rasnic Tem. Denver, CO: Umbral Press, 1982, paper, p. 117-118.

D29. "The Accident," in *Orangewood* 3 (Spring, 1978): 20.

D30. "Prose," in *Orangewood* 3 (Spring, 1978): 19.

D31. "Behavior During Plague," in *Chowder Review* 10/11 (Autumn/ Winter, 1978-1979): 69.

D32. "Hymn," in *Chowder Review* 10/11 (Autumn/Winter, 1978-1979): 71.

D33. "Life with Them," in *Chowder Review* 10/11 (Autumn/Winter, 1978-1979): 70.

D34. "Mutual Brother," in *Italia America* 4 (January-June, 1979): 47.

D35. "Religion Three," in *Italia America* 4 (January-June, 1979): 47.

D36. "The Road As Built," in *Italia America* 4 (January-June, 1979): 47.

D37. "Telling a Truth," in *Italia America* 4 (January-June, 1979): 47.

16

D38. "Three Levels of Reader Interest," in *Italia America* 4 (January-June, 1979): 47.

D39. "The Accident," in *Quarterly West* 9 (Spring/Summer, 1979): 72-73.

D40. "Forcing a Love Poem," in *Zanja Review* 1 (Spring, 1980): 64.

D41. "More," in *Zanja Review* 1 (Spring, 1980): 63.

D42. "What We Have Around Us," in *Zanja Review* 1 (Spring, 1980): 62.

D43. "Party," in *Southwest Review* 65 (Autumn, 1980): 383-384.

D44. "Parents," in *Zanja Review* 3 (Spring, 1982): 46.

GRAPHIC/EXPERIMENTAL WORK

E1.   "Greeting Card Idea #2," in *Fifth Assembling: A Collection of Otherwise Unpublishable Manuscripts*, edited by Richard Kostelanetz, Henry Korn, and Mike Metz.   Brooklyn, NY: Assembling Press, 1974, paper, p. 173.

E2.   "Hot Tamales," in *Fifth Assembling: A Collection of Otherwise Unpublishable Manuscripts*, edited by Richard Kostelanetz, Henry Korn, and Mike Metz. Brooklyn, NY: Assembling Press, 1974, paper, p. 174.

E3.   "A Holographic Documentary," in *West Coast Poetry Review* 4 (Winter, 1974): 5-13.

18

PAPERS

F1. *Planning Environment Report for the Southern California Earthquake Safety Advisory Board*, by Bruce McAllister, Richard Stuart Olson, Douglas Nilson, and Linda Nilson. Redlands, CA: Policy Research Center, University of Redlands, 1981, 141 p., paper.

F2. *Eagle Center Master Plan*, by Bruce McAllister with various consultants. Produced by three consulting firms: Agbabian Associates, TEMJAM Industries, and VSP Associates. San Bernardino, CA: County of San Bernardino, January, 1985, 175 p., paper.

F3. *Eagle Center Principal Prospectus*, by Bruce McAllister with Michael Terpin. San Bernardino, CA: County of San Bernardino, January, 1985, 22 p., paper.

EDITORIAL POSTS

G1.   Overseas Editor, *Cave* 1 (April, 1972).   Dunedin, New Zealand: Caveman Press. [literary magazine]

G2.   Associate Editor, *West Coast Poetry Review*, 1972-1977. [literary magazine]

Founded in 1970 as a literary quarterly specializing in conventional and experimental poetry, *WCPR* began its editorial direction under William Fox (Publisher and Editor) and Bruce McAllister (Associate Editor) in 1972.   The publication ceased in 1979. McAllister worked on the following issues:

        a.   Vol. I, No. 4/Vol. 2, No. 1—Summer/Fall, 1972
        b.   Vol. II, No. 2—Winter, 1972/73
        c.   Vol. II, No. 3—Spring, 1973
        d.   Vol. III, No. 2—Winter, 1973
        e.   Vol. III, No. 3—Spring, 1974
        f.   Vol. III, No. 4—Summer, 1974
        g.   Vol. IV, Nos. 1-2—Fall, 1974
        h.   Vol. V, No. 1—1976
        i.   Vol. V, No. 2—1977

G3.   Associate (and Fiction) Editor, West Coast   Poetry Review Press, Reno, Nevada, 1973-1982. [book series]

a.   *Weathering*, by Duane Ackerson. 1973.
b.   *Poems: Massman, Costanzo, McAllister.* 1973
c.   *A Problem of High Water*, by Greg Kuzma. 1973.
d.   *Leaves and Ashes*, by John Haines.   1974.   [Co-published with Kayak Books, Santa Cruz, CA]
e.   *Cage with Only One Side*, by Enrique Anderson Imbert, translated by Isabel Reade. 1974.
f.   *Going Places*, by William Stafford. 1974.
g.   *The Road to Tamazunchale*, by Ron Arias. 1975.   Also released as Vol. IV, No. 4 of *West Coast Poetry Review*.
h.   *Me Too*, by Raymond Federman. 1975.
i.   *Selected Ponds*, by Ian Hamilton Finlay, with selected photos by Dave Paterson. 1975.
j.   *Ground Zero*, by Thomas Johnson. 1975.
k.   *Constructs/Stories*, by Richard Kostelanetz. 1975.
l.   *The Schoolhouse Poems*, by Joanne de Longchamps. 1975.
m.   *Softwhere, Inc.*, by Aaron Marcus. 1975.

n. *Lessons in Alchemy,* by George Hitchcock. 1976.
o. *Skin: Shadows, Silence,* by Deena Metzger. 1976.
p. *Winning at Poker and Games of Chance.* 1977.
q. *One Creature,* by Joanne de Longchamps. 1977.
r. *On the Ward,* by Don Gordon. 1977.
s. *Poems from the Fifth Season,* by d. s. long; *Forest,* by David Cheer. 1977.
t. *Ronald Davis at (the) University of Nevada,* Church Fine Arts Gallery, March 11 to April 8, 1977. 1977.
u. *Nancy Grossman, University of Nevada, Reno,* Church Fine Arts Gallery, January 6-31, 1978. 1978.
v. *Excavations,* by Don Gordon. 1979.
w. *Visual Literature Criticism,* edited by Richard Kostelanetz. Also released as Vol. V, No. 3 of *West Coast Poetry Review.* 1979.
x. *Their Immortal Hearts,* edited by Bruce McAllister. 1980.
y. *Warm Bloods, Cold Bloods,* by Joanne de Longchamps. 1981.
z. *Softwhere, Inc., Vol. 2,* by Aaron Marcus. 1982.

G4. Academic Affairs Editor, *Bulletin of the Science Fiction Writers of America,* Sea Cliff, NY, 1973-1974. [professional journal]

    a. Vol. IX, Nos. 2/3—Summer, 1973
    b. Vol. IX, No. 4—Fall, 1973
    c. Vol. IX, No. 5—1974
    d. Vol. X, No. 2—Fall, 1974

G5. Guest Editor, *Edge* (Autumn-Winter, 1973), published by Edge Press, Christ Church, New Zealand. This volume, a "speculative literature" anthology, was also issue 5/6 of *SF Directions.* [literary magazine]

G6. Managing Editor, *Best SF* anthology series, edited by Brian Aldiss and Harry Harrison, 1973-1975. [book series]

a. *Best SF: 1973.* New York: G. P. Putnam's Sons, 1974, 238 p., cloth.
ab. as: *The 7th Annual Best SF: 73.* New York: Berkley Books, 1974, 255 p., paper.
b. *Best SF 1974.* Indianapolis: Bobbs-Merrill Co., 1975, 253 p., cloth.
c. *Best SF: 75, the Ninth Annual.* Indianapolis: Bobbs-Merrill Co., 1976, 240 p., cloth.
cb. as: *The Year's Best Science Fiction #9.* London: Futura Books, 1976, 206 p., paper.

G7. Contributing Editor, *Italia America,* published by Italia

America, South San Francisco, CA, 1978-1979.   [literary magazine]

MEDIA APPEARANCES

H1.   Panelist, *Science Fiction Hour*, KPFK-FM (radio station), Los Angeles, CA, 1973.

H2.   Panelist on fiction and poetry, *Twentieth Century Dialogues*, KVCR-TV, San Bernardino, CA, 1977.

AWARDS AND PRIZES

I1.   Between 1967-1985, the following stories, novelettes, and novellas were recommended for the Nebula Award, although none reached the final ballot: "Benji's Pencil," "Ecce Femina!" "Prime-Time Teaser," "Victor," "What He Wore For Them," "When the Fathers Go," and "Their Immortal Hearts," "The Ark."

I2.   Scholar in Poetry, Bread Loaf Writers Conference, 1972.

I3.   Fellow in Fiction, Squaw Valley Writers Conference, 1973.

I4.   Professor of the Year, University of Redlands, 1978.

I5.   Judge, College Literary Magazine Competition, National Endowment for the Arts, 1979-1980.

I6.   Faculty Teaching Award, University of Redlands, 1982.

ABOUT THE AUTHOR

J1.   *Billion Year Spree: The True History of Science Fiction*, by
       Brian Aldiss.   Garden City, NY: Doubleday & Co., 1973,
       cloth, p. 304. [critique]

J2.   "McAllister, Bruce," in *Contemporary Authors*, Vol. 33-36,
       edited by Ann Evory.   Detroit: Gale Research Co., 1973?,
       cloth, p.   . [biography]

J3.   "McAllister, Bruce," in *Who's Who in the West*, 15th Edi-
       tion, 1976-1977.   Chicago: Marquis Who's Who, 1976, cloth,
       p. 475. [biography]

J4.   "McAllister, Bruce," in *Contemporary Authors, First Revi-
       sion*, Vol. 33-36, edited by Ann Evory.   Detroit: Gale
       Research Co., 1978, cloth, p. 201. [biography]

J5.   *Encyclopedia of Science Fiction*, edited by Robert Hold-
       stock.   London: Octopus Books, 1978, cloth, p. 168.   [cri-
       tique]

J6.   "McAllister, Bruce," in *Who's Who in the West*, 16th Edi-
       tion, 1978-1979.   Chicago: Marquis Who's Who, 1978, cloth,
       p. 467. [biography]

J7.   "Professor of the Year," in *Redlands Report* 9 (Summer,
       1979): 2.

J8.   "McAllister, Bruce," in *The Science Fiction Encyclopedia*,
       edited by Peter Nicholls.   Garden City, NY: Doubleday &
       Co., 1979, cloth, p. 368. [critical biography]

J9.   "McAllister, Bruce," in *Science Fiction and Fantasy Litera-
       ture*, by R. Reginald.   Detroit: Gale Research Co., 1979,
       cloth, Vol. 2, p. 993-994. [bio-bibliography]

J10.   "McAllister, Bruce," in   *Who's Who in the West*, 17th Edi-
       tion, 1980-1981.   Chicago: Marquis Who's Who, 1980, cloth,
       p. 476. [biography]

J11.   "McAllister, Bruce," in *A Directory of American Poets and
       Fiction Writers: 1983-84*.   New York: Poets and Writers,
       1983, cloth, p. 22. [biography]

FORTHCOMING:

J12.   "McAllister, Bruce,"   in *Twentieth Century Science Fiction
       Writers*, 2nd ed., edited by Curtis C. Smith.   London: St.
       James, 1986, cloth, p.   . [critique]

CRITICAL COMMENTS

"Bruce McAllister has quietly become, in the last fifteen years, one of the most interesting and rewarding of science fiction writers. His stories combine the excitement of new ideas with a careful and thoughtful attention to the realities of science, and how to present them in effective, exciting ways."

—Terry Carr

HUMANITY PRIME

"*Humanity Prime* must be a contender for the best first novel of the year. Written by a highly talented writer in his early twenties, it is a reminder that science fiction can apply equally well to the less precise sciences of biology and psychology. It is refreshing to know that there is quality science fiction still being written..."

—*Science Fiction News*

"McAllister has written a marvellous first novel that presents a society of another kind--still human, but aquatic. This beautiful description of a solitary race utterly lacking in a mechanical civlization, but enjoying a depth of communication unknown to us, leaves one with the feeling that if there is a society of intelligent porpoises in Earth's seas, it must be something like this."

—Dennis Livingston, *Futures*

"THEIR IMMORTAL HEARTS"

"A complex *tour de force* which conveys a feeling of strange, vast spans of time, and creates a genuinely different future. A superior piece of fiction, it could well become a landmark story of this decade."

—Gregory Benford

TITLE INDEX

"The Accident," D29, D39
"After the Bomb Cliches," B12
"Aging," D6
"Aligning Constellations and Pets," D24
"And So Say All of Us," B11
"Ark, The," B41
"The Arrangement," B19
"Autohuman 14," B9

"Baby," B44
"Behavior During Plague," D31
"Benji's Pencil," B6
Best SF: 1973 (editor), G6a
Best SF: 1974 (editor), G6b
Best SF: 75, the Ninth Annual (editor), G6c
"The Big Boy," B8
"Boy," B34
"Breasts," D20
Bulletin of the Science Fiction Writers of America (editor), G4

Cage with Only One Side (editor), G3e
"Cauchemar de Sabel," B4b
Cave (editor), G1
"Clichés Nucléaires," B12b
Constructs/Stories (editor), G3k
"Cottage with White Picket Fence," B31
"Des Crayons pour Benji," B6d

"Do We Need This Knowledge?" C3
Dream Baby (novel), A8
"Dream Baby" (story), B45

"E Pluribus Solo," B13
Eagle Center Master Plan, F2
Eagle Center Principal Prospectus, F3
"Ecce Femina!" B17
Edge (editor), G5
"Eleven Days Without Sleep," C1
Excavations (editor), G3v
"Exploring Late," D2

"Le Facce Dietro il Vetro," B1c
The Faces Outside (collection), A4
"The Faces Outside" (story), B1

www.ingramcontent.com/pod-product-compliance
Lightning Source LLC
Chambersburg PA
CBHW030031290326
41934CB00005B/571